Forever TRUCKIN

Mastering The Will To Win

Eddie "Truck" Gordon and Meiyoko Taylor

TABLE OF CONTENTS

ACKNOWLEDGEMENTS

It's hard to attain success without surrounding yourself with great positive people. There are many people who have played and continue to play a key role in my growth as a human being.

First and foremost, I want to thank my family and friends. I want to acknowledge my mother and father for laying the bricks to my foundation as a man. Watching all the sacrifices you two made for us kids was paramount to my future success. I want to thank my big brother Julian for leading by example and always giving me tough love. I want to thank my sister Claudia for being by my side through the good, bad, and the ugly. To my second family, the Huggins. You truly are my home away from home. Della, you're my second mom and the love of my life. Gideon and Josh you two are my brothers from another mother. The memories we have are endless and continue to grow.

I want to give a special thanks to my ex-wife Gloria. We have been through the good, bad, and indifferent. The life lessons we have learned from each other prepared us for life. Thank you for the best gift, our sons D'Angelo and Jayden.

It's obvious by now we all know that behind every good man there is a strong woman. To my fiancée and future wife Stella, I am so lucky to have you in my life. Thank you for believing in me and supporting me through think & thin. Thank you for giving me two amazing boys, Marquis and Jaxson. They complete our family of six for now. However, who knows what the future brings!

To my boys, D'Angelo, Marquis, Jayden, and Jaxson. You guys are the air in my lungs and the reason I breathe. You are all my WHY. All of you are the reason I get up and do everything I do. Thank you for your love and support.

I have to thank a few special men in my life. First my coaches Russ Cellan, Joe Chetti, Keith Brown, Steve Whelan, Dave Gordon, Matt Serra, Ray Longo, and Eric Hyer. You men taught me how to be a good student, coach, man, and most importantly, a good father. You all led by example. I was always treated like I was your very own and this is exactly how I treat the kids I coach today. Whether you know it or not, you guys are truly my backbone.

Last but not least, no way any of this is possible without one of the most humble and considerate men to walk this earth! That man is my good friend and mentor Mr. Matthew Proman. You are a brother to me. When no one else believed in me, you did. When I lost belief in myself at some of the darkest moments in my life you were always there. Without you I don't know where and what I would be doing. Some people talk about how much they care but you my friend, show how much you care. I just want to thank you for giving me your heart and soul. For that I am forever grateful and indebted to you.

Thank you to all who have supported me through this amazing life. It is far from over. I express my sincere appreciation and gratitude from the bottom of my heart!

INTRODUCTION

My life has been far from easy but it has built me in to the man I am today. I've had ups, downs, trials, tribulations, disappointments and many successes. However, it is all these things that separate the people who wait for things to happen from those who actually make things happen. With passion, heart, and perseverance comes an inner strength that will lead to success in whatever you choose to do in this lifetime. In this book you are going to be learning about the mentality I have developed throughout my life. This mentality has been the reason for my success and it continues to drive me daily. Planted inside all of us is a seed of greatness. In order for that seed to grow it needs to be watered and cultivated so that we can maximize our greatest potential. I am here to tell you that it's never too late to water that seed. Success truly has no age limit and I believe we owe it to the world to share the wonderful gifts that make us extraordinary. Prepare to be taken on a journey throughout the incredible life that I have been blessed to live thus far. You are about to learn how I used all of my mistakes, adversities and failures to push myself into a life of success that I could have never imagined. I have become a UFC champion, successful businessman, father to the most amazing children, Emmy award winner, and I know many more wonderful things lie ahead for me. However, I would have never made it if I didn't go through the fire of adversity. The challenge of being told I could not change my life's path, my UFC/TUF career and tragic events in my personal life, further nourished my determination to succeed. It was because of those difficult stages, that I was able to unlock my full potential and embrace who I truly am. I am happy, I am healthy and I am wealthy. You have the ability within you right now to create these same results in your life.

This snapshot of my life along with the 6 very important principles within these pages will help highlight and showcase some ways to improve your mindset. Your greatness deserves to shine upon the rest of the world. I believe in you. May this book guide you to becoming all that you are capable of being and may you always remember to keep on "truckin" your way to success!

CHAPTER 1 : WHERE IT ALL STARTED

HUMBLE BEGINNINGS

Hardships and family played a huge role in molding my life. I was born in Jamaica West Indies raised by my mother and father. I am the youngest of seven children and was definitely the runt of the litter. I was a tiny scrappy boy with a big heart. There has been a fighter inside of me since the day I was born. Back then I had to fight for everything including meals because there were so many of us. My parents were blue collar workers and they made sure to instill hard work in our mindset. Desiring a much better life for us, they decided to migrate to America to give our large family the best chance to succeed. I was only three years old at the time we left Jamaica. I remember my mother telling me that we were leaving our home in Jamaica and the fear that filled my heart was overwhelming. For the first time in my life I had experienced fear of the unknown. Not knowing what was to come next absolutely terrified me. As a little guy, all I knew was that my current life was safe and secure. I did not want to step outside of my comfort zone but my parents had much bigger dreams for us. My Father traveled to America before us. He was a cabinet maker and very good with his hands. He worked day and night till he established a solid foundation for us in America. Once he settled in and saved enough money, he sent for us to join him in America. I don't remember exactly what was going through my head that very moment when we got off the plane. However, what I do remember is the chilling cold and my first experience seeing snow! I began to look at the green ground covered in this white heavy cold fluff. That was my welcome to the concrete jungle and one of the most popular places on the planet, New York.

My mom and dad were determined to give us a better life than what they had experienced. We were far from wealthy, we had little money, and it was extremely hard growing up. As children we didn't always get what we wanted but we always had what we needed. Our upbringing made us grateful for the little things in life. In those days we were too young to understand why things were this way. We often wondered why other kids in school could wear the hottest new brand name sneakers and we never owned a pair. We didn't understand how these cool fashions we desired to have always seemed to skip our household. I remember wearing my jeans tucked over my pay less attack force sneakers hoping no one would notice that they were not Nikes. I remember not being able to join the expensive sport leagues because my parents had to pay to keep our lights on instead of paying for little league baseball registration. I remember going to the first day of junior high school with a baldy haircut because I had to cut my own hair. Although I needed a haircut, my parents were unable to afford that either. However, one of the richest and most valuable things our family did have was love. It was so hard to fit in because we were so different from everyone else. We had different accents, we didn't dress like everyone else, and we were always the new kids on the block. Our family bounced from town to town until we finally settled in Freeport which is in Long Island New York. I couldn't have asked for a better environment to flourish and develop as a man. Freeport was where my destiny began to unfold. This was the beginning of it all. From struggles to accomplishments, all those moments in time were just the beginning of my much needed evolution.

MY ROLE MODEL

As a child I carried the biggest chip on my shoulder. Even as I grew older I was still a tiny scrawny kid with a ton of heart and I felt like I had so much to prove. My older brother set high expectations for all of us due to his many accomplishments. His accomplishments always made me feel like I had to push myself even more in everything I did and I still have that mentality today. My brother was my idol and role model growing up. He was one of the best athletes I have ever seen and he seemed to excel at everything. I was always Julian's little brother. For years I was ok with that, but as I got older the desire to have my own identity began to grow. My big brother never put any pressure on me socially or athletically. Although my brother never placed that pressure on me I still put that pressure on myself. I always wanted to make Julian proud. I often sought for his acceptance even though I always had it. Competing internally with myself to match his greatness became common and was key to developing my drive to be great.

My brother Julian is responsible for helping me become the man I am today and was the originator of my nickname. They say a name makes a man and I couldn't agree more. Some kids wanted to be Barry Sanders or Bo Jackson growing up, but I wanted to be Julian! I remember wearing my brothers football jersey and playing football with his friends. It definitely fueled my drive and confidence just to be worthy enough to play on the field with them. It didn't matter how tiny I was. My hunger for winning and competing started to become noticeable above others. I played Running Back and I was trampling over the older kids one after another. From that day on, my brother called me Truck and it stuck with me from the 4th grade until this present day. At first I hated the nickname. I thought it was stupid, pointless and I literally weighed 110lbs soaking wet. To me it wasn't sexy or cool but it was from my big brother so eventually I grew into the name. Realizing later on that it was more than something people used to identify me, I learned that "Truck" is a mindset and it has become a way of life for me. When I encounter obstacles or adversity I turn them into opportunities and I keep on Truckin. Everything is not always going to go your way. The key is to work hard and truck through every obstacle so you can achieve a life of greatness. The nickname Truck defines my life's journey which includes every success and failure. In my life's darkest moments, it has given me the confidence to keep pushing forward.

Although my exterior was always strong in order to protect myself, I still always had a warm soft interior. I was adamant about guarding the soft spoken mild mannered individual beneath the surface. From a very young age I would put my heart and trust into believing that everyone had good within them. There have been times in my life that this thinking has resulted in being hurt and taken advantage of. The Truck mindset was formed not because of a want, but because of a need. The need to succeed, the need for protection, the need to rise, and the need to strive towards excellence made this mindset a reality. There comes a point where you reach a crossroad in your life and you will either sink or swim. I made the decision to swim with everything I had, and I am still swimming today.

Principle #1

Your background, size, age, color, or current situation does not matter. If you have the desire to succeed and you make the choice to take action, you too can be great. Success has NO age limit.

CHAPTER 2 : A FIRE KINDLED

High school is a turning point for most young people and I was no exception. This is the point in life where you will make choices that will shape your character in the present and for years to come. During my high school years I excelled academically and as an athlete. It was not because I was the smartest kid, the fastest, or the most athletic. I just made a conscious decision that I would truck through anything in my way. As a High school student I was a dreamer like most kids. I dreamt with my eyes wide open, set my goals high, and believed that I would do great things in life. Kids and teachers would often laugh at my goals saying that they were impossible. At times they would even laugh right in my face. In my head nothing was impossible if I was dedicated and I put forth the effort to achieve it. When teachers would ask what I wanted to be when I grew up I would say "I will be a professional athlete." To me that was my destiny and my future. I was certain that I would be a professional football player trucking my way right into the NFL. Even though friends, teachers, and almost everyone laughed or doubted me, I never stopped believing it was possible. I refused to let their perception of me be my reality. At night I would sit up and sign my signature to a blank piece of paper. I would do this over and over until my hand got tired, knowing in my heart that it would be worth something one day. While the world laughed I persevered and eventually my beliefs along with my hard work paid off. In my junior year while playing football in Freeport High School, we lost the last game of the season which knocked us out of the playoffs. I was absolutely devastated. At that moment as I walked off the field crying and disheartened, I made the decision to rewrite the history books at Freeport. I made up my mind that I would do everything in my power to do what no other Freeport football team has ever done which was win a Long Island Class 1 football championship. In the off season when I told people we would win it all next year, they laughed like it was a pipe dream but boy were they wrong! I found that even some of the closest people to me who should have been my biggest supporters, were not. This added fuel to the fire within me as everyone kept piling up doubt on top of doubt. Every minute of every second in the offseason was spent pouring my heart and soul into my craft. I was determined to lead by example and to carry my fellow team of young men to the promise land. Each moment of every workout and sprint was the foundation of what I envisioned and that was to take home a long Island class 1 football championship.

A VISION REALIZED

Just as I had envisioned, a few games and a few months later we were knocking on the door of greatness. The time was here and our team was undefeated. On the field we dominated other football teams that beat us the year prior. Our undefeated regular season led us to the Long Island Championship game vs. another undefeated team, the Commack Cougars. It was an epic game that decades later still goes down as one of the greatest games in Long Island's football history. That game was a back and forth war! It went all the way into overtime and the game came down to one play. We scored and then kicked the extra point. Commack answered back with a touchdown of their own but they decided to go for the win. This one play was standing in the way of my vision being realized and everything that I said we would achieve. Commack then lined up for the

2pt conversion and the chance to win the game. I remember like it was yesterday. Our high school hall of fame Coach Russ Cellan called a time out. He brought the team into the huddle shared a clear and powerful statement to us all. He said "Ok men. Yes I said men. You guys are no longer boys. This is the last play of the game and someone has to make a play. We are going to win or lose this game on this play. What's it going to be?" The whistle blows and the time out is over. The referee brings us back on the field for the final play. The crowd is screaming so loud it became deafening. The message was clear. Someone on our team had to make a play. The ball is snapped and the play is in full swing. For the first time in my life everything began to move in slow motion. I, Truck Gordon, exploded through the line of scrimmage, ripped through a potential blocker, and grabbed the quarter back who was rolling to his right. With one long extended arm I had sacked the 1st team all-state Commack quarterback to end an iconic game for the ages. The crowd exploded, everyone rushed the field in chaotic glory, and right then, I achieved what everyone thought was impossible. My mission was complete. Freeport's first championship in history was in the record books. All of my many critics were immediately silenced. From that moment my belief in myself was at an all-time high and I had faith that I could accomplish anything I set my mind to. In my heart I know anything can be accomplished if you believe in yourself and gear your actions towards that specific goal. That day set me up for the rest of my life validating that you should always believe in yourself even when nobody else does.

What started out in high school as a spark of passion developed into a burning flame. Some people fold and crumble when adversity is sitting at their door steps. Others rise up and excel. I chose to rise above the doubters and naysayers. I used their negative energy to better myself and the people around me. No matter how strong your fire is there will always be people that will try to extinguish it. Never let them. Always be aware of the fact that we all are perfectly imperfect.

There is a spark that rests inside of every one of us. It is up to you to find it. When you do it will lead you towards your greatness and when darkness strikes, that fire will burn as bright as it's ever been.

Principle #2

Someone's opinion of you does not have to be your reality. Believe in your vision. Ignite the fire within you and the impossible will soon become possible!

CHAPTER 3 : IN THE FACE OF ADVERSITY

Continuing my dream to be in the NFL, I started playing division 1 college football for the Fordham Rams. The rich history of Fordham football includes the great Vince Lombardi and the seven blocks of granite. I kept truckin at Fordham, working hard on and off the field. I was a scholar athlete at Fordham gaining academic all-American honors. Being at Fordham was no easy task. There were many ups and downs just like everywhere else. My whole life consisted of working and pushing myself to be great. What I was unaware of coming from High school football to division 1 football was the mental and physical toll that comes from being in a sports environment. It really started to affect me physically and even more so, mentally. My freshman year was full of road blocks, tears, smiles and more adversity. It was a roller coaster of emotions. However, no day equaled the historical day that would soon come. The day I am referring to was September 11th, 2001. It seemed like any other day but on that day the entire country would come under attack. It impacted the great state of New York and every state in America. The inhumane terrorist attacks were felt around the world. Being in the heart of New York at the time was a dramatic, scary and heart wrenching experience. Our lives were forever impacted that day as a country. My friends and I were mourning, scared to death, and confused. Our coaches decided it would be in our team's best interest to practice later that day because we were playing another rival New York Division 1 football team, the Columbia University Lions.

I had many mixed emotions about practicing that day for multiple reasons but our leader was Coach and he makes the decisions. We as players just did what was expected of us.

DEVASTATING NEWS

As practice went on my heart was not in it and that day ended up being twice as devastating for me. Today would be the day I suffered the worst injury in my football and athletic career. My ligaments were torn in my knee and I wasn't sure if I had a future in athletics after that massive setback. Not only was I nervous, I was terrified and I felt sorry for myself. It was one of the loneliest feelings I ever had at the time. I think it was symbolic that I got hurt on 9/11 because while I was feeling sorry for myself, I had friends and teammates who were missing. They were lost, hurt or could possibly be dead. So, I had to put my pride behind me and be grateful that I had air in my lungs. I then wiped the tears away from my eyes and I made a promise to myself to work until I was back better than ever. I knew it wasn't going to be easy but I was going to truck on through. Some days were better than others but every day was an opportunity to get healthier mentally and physically. I surpassed all expectations I had set forth for myself and became a two-time captain of the Fordham Rams football team. What a great feeling it was helping the Rams win the first Patriot League Championship in university history! For me personally, it was even more satisfying of a feeling because so many people questioned my decision to attend Fordham. Few believed I could win a D1 championship while being there. To achieve that with my teammates who knew we could win was a glorious victory in itself. While the world may have mocked my goals, my beliefs and actions helped me push through. Once again my hard work turned my sweat into smiles. I was finally able to relish in my success. However, it was very brief and I was unprepared for what was next in my football career. After graduating college my dreams seemed to slip away slowly. I wasn't getting many offers from NFL teams and it angered me because I knew I was good enough to play. I could compete with athletes at the highest level. I became quite discouraged but I used that anger to fuel the truck and kept on moving toward a different route.

Months after graduating Fordham, I got married to my high school sweet heart. I had decided to put my dreams on the back burner. Actually, it was more like the shelf way back in the garage. Being newly married, I began working in corporate America entering the rat race. At the time I felt as though that was the right thing to do. I left the football field behind me and we started a beautiful family. There were many good years but it felt like a piece of me was missing. I still had that competitive hunger burning within me but flames felt as if they were extinguished with my current lifestyle at this point. As beautiful as my life seemed from the outside, it was falling apart from the inside and my marriage began to unravel. The happy go lucky dreamer I used to be was nowhere to be found and everything became overwhelming for me. The fact that I wasn't the father I hoped to be hurt me even more. I was losing pieces of myself daily being suffocated by my own shortcomings. In the midst of our young marriage, my wife and I started growing apart. As time went on we became more and more distant. We eventually grew into the people we were meant to be. Unfortunately we had become strangers to one another. This transition was a heart breaking experience. My happiness had deteriorated and so did every other aspect of my life. Shortly after, my health was next. I went from a Division 1 athlete to a 300 pound overweight, unhealthy, and white collar husband of two kids. My spirit was completely broken. As my happiness and health diminished, my wealth did also. I had officially hit rock bottom and nothing was the way it was supposed to be.

WHEN IT RAINS IT POURS

My life had broken down from the inside out and lost my sense of direction. Within time, I started to make horrible decisions and lost touch with reality. Not even a glimmer of happiness was present. I didn't know who I was anymore, I felt alone, and I hid my emotions from the people closest to me. I was very good at hiding my pain and just going through the motions of life even though on the inside I was screaming to get out of the mess I created. The bad decisions that were made during this dark moment in my life soon resulted in legal trouble. Throughout this time my judgement became cloudy and I continued to make bad choices. These choices only put me further in a hole. Supporting my family financially was still my main priority but there came a time when things really spiraled out of control. My wife and I lived a very privileged life like most young successful people. The problem however, is that we lived above our means. I thought I had it taken care of but that couldn't be further from the truth. To lose control over everything was very hard for me to fathom to say the least. First thing to go was my health. Then, the misery assisted me in gaining an enormous amount of weight. After my health the next to suffer was our financial stability and that added further damage to our home life. My wife was always used to getting what she wanted as far as clothes, shoes, gifts and cars. She definitely was a recipient of the finer things in life. Being in finance, everyone felt the financial shock of the market crashing and some of the worst financial downturns in history. Some people were able to manage financially better than others. I thought we were holding off well but I was definitely mistaken. My wife's shopping habits did not slow down with the down turn of the market and she racked up a ton of maxed out credit cards like most Americans. She was always diligent paying the bills so I assumed everything was under control but that wasn't reality. The ugly truth was that she was draining us dry. I was so upset for being mentally out of it for so long. I was blind to the fact that she had a shopping addiction and I never noticed any pattern or any crazy spending escapades. Then one day for no apparent reason, I decided to open one of her credit cards which was totally out of character for me. What I uncovered next took my breath completely away.

To my surprise, when I viewed the credit card statement it showed that the card was maxed out $15,000 and she was paying 29.99 percent interest. My heart dropped to my stomach and I immediately became anxious. As a finance guy all I could see was thousands of dollars in interest fees being wasted away. I was now on high alert. I went through every credit card statement and discovered that each one was similar to the first shocking revelation. Maxed out credit limits were on every piece of plastic. Filled with so much anger and frustration, I was ready to implode. I got my emotions together and that night we had a much needed heart to heart discussion. My conclusion was to try and correct our financial crisis hoping it would result in a better life. Using the money in our savings account, I paid off every card available. It was then established that we would not use credit cards unless it was an absolute emergency. I honestly blamed myself for not noticing this disaster and being completely caught up in my own feelings. Moving forward, I kept a much closer eye on our finances.

A few months went by and it seems as though her spending was under control with no shopping sprees in sight. Once again being foolish and naïve, I thought that I solved the problem. Unfortunately, again I was mistaken. I stopped supervising our credit because I was preoccupied with other important things and the same thing happened again! This time I was alerted with a phone call from the credit card company informing me that I missed a payment on a credit card. This was a credit card that I never knew existed. I was furious, upset, angry, and sad all over again. How could I let this happen not once but twice? I felt like a total failure. What could I possibly do to dig us out of this hole again only a few months after our first economic crisis? I knew that I needed a solution and I needed it fast. My finance instincts kicked in and I began looking for another solution to our financial struggles. I was always offered side jobs and consulting opportunities from clients that I met but I always turned them down. After all, money was not an issue at those times. Since I had become so desperate to make this issue go away, I made a decision that would create an even bigger problem for me in the future. I started to work for one of my clients off the books. My job was as a financial consultant for their firm. It was good money and it was easy. Deep down inside I knew this easy money was too good to be true. Something just didn't feel right and you should always trust your instincts. My gut was telling me to run. The current Ponzi schemes were still fresh and the financial crisis in the market was still riding strong. The feelings that this company was shady ran all through my veins. The CEO of the company offered me a great sum of money to walk away from my current financial institution to work full time for them and play a larger role in their company. As much as I may have wanted to take the monetary upgrade, my gut said no way. The best and only right decision I made in this dark phase of my life was turning that proposal down. I had a talk with a friend and trusted advisor who suggested I sever all ties with the company. Their business model seemed really skeptical. I took their advice and parted ways. I was now off to look for something else. Ironically, that company was under investigation by the FBI. Before long it was raided and completely shut down for business. Turning down that big pay day was a life saver. However, I still had to pay for my mistakes. Since I was a paid consultant, I had to pay back all the money I got paid in commissions plus interest. This was another gigantic shot to my finances, my life, and my marriage. In my youth and at this time in my life, I did not use good judgement. Being young, dumb, and naive is an understatement. My judgement was poor and I allowed a temporary moment in my life to control important decisions. A temporary problem almost ruined what I took a life time to build. Ultimately, I had no one else to blame for my short comings but myself. I admit now that I am actually grateful for those obstacles in life because without them I would not be the man I am today Eventually, I made some adjustments and didn't allow those dark moments in my life to totally consume me.

Principle #3

Never let your emotions control your decision making. They will wreak havoc on your personal, professional, and financial well-being. Control your emotions. Don't let them control you.

CHAPTER 4 : THE BREAKTHROUGH

THE ENCOURAGEMENT I NEEDED

During those dark periods in my life I was willing to help everyone else but myself and I needed help the most I was too afraid to let anyone down. It became the norm to sacrifice my sanity and happiness for the sake of others. Soon the walls started to close in on me and I needed to get out. I had to detoxify my life and I had to take inventory of everyone I allowed in it. I decided to make one of the hardest decisions I had ever made in my life. My mind and heart led me to separate from the woman I thought I would spend the rest of my life with. My former beloved high school sweetheart would now become my ex-wife. This was definitely not how I saw my life turning out but I had no other choice. My life needed to be fixed from the inside out and that started with the people closest to me. What came after was another very hard choice. I never imagined having to ever move out of my home but that's what I did. For the first time in my life I was away from my kids which brought me to the lowest feeling I ever experienced. I was dealing with a divorce, legal problems, self-inflicted drama, and being away from my own children. These were all scary emotional issues within themselves. Dealing with them all at once was debilitating. I continued to put my usual external facade of happiness on while I continued to slowly die inside. It had gotten so bad that I no longer wanted to leave my house. The entire world came crashing down on me.

I was officially an emotional wreck. I felt like I failed in marriage, work, fatherhood, and life. Everything was at a standstill and I was in a state of disbelief for months. I needed to sit and speak to someone who knew me because I could no longer pretend nor could I hold this pain in any longer. Only one person in the entire world saw the pain behind my smile and it was time to see her. I made time to go visit the closest woman to me. It was finally time to visit my world, my place of comfort, and of unconditional love. It was time to see my mother.

I sat down with my mom and as always, she saw right through my exterior. At that moment I broke down in tears pouring out my heart and soul to her. Doing so made me feel like I could breathe again. To hear the words come out my mother's mouth, "you're a great man and a great father" made all the difference in the world. She then said "We all make mistakes in life. I love you son." Those brief words restored me and brought me back to reality. My passion began to stir inside of me once again and I became determined to get back on track. The foundation that was formed and instilled in since my childhood was still there after the storm passed. I was a great man, a great person, and more importantly, I believed it again. I was and I still am Truck. I'd rise above my adversities, Truck through my problems, and would always make those adversities my advantages. I took back control of my life and developed an even stronger mindset of greatness. My life had ups and downs but these experiences shaped me forever. I learned that with the right mindset we can achieve far greater than we could ever imagine. Everyone has that special something inside of them. We just have to use the experiences that take place in our lives to tap into that greatness and become who we were meant to be.

To know where we are going, I feel we must understand where we come from. Our lives can either be a tragic saga of events or an adventurous tale in which we conquer whatever was dragging us down. Where we come from is the beginning of our story and although you can't rewrite the past you can always expand on your future. Your story is simply the foundation of your mindset which can be molded into where you want your life to be. The only person who chooses the ending is you so take that power and put it towards greatness.

Some of that power is focus, hard work, dedication and motivation. I simply don't believe in luck. I am not a leprechaun, I'm not short, and I'm not green. From the day I came into this world, all I knew was how to work hard and that was the foundation that has been engraved in my soul. My parents built that work ethic for our family through actions and it spoke volumes growing up. Each day they worked hard and excelled while I watched them closely. This gave me such a great admiration for my parents. No matter what obstacle they faced, they approached it with so much confidence, perseverance, and mental toughness. There is a powerful quote that's been heard around the world. "How you do anything is how you do Everything." I live my life with great belief in those words. The funny thing is that before I ever heard or read that quote, my immigrant parents had that mindset and had already passed it on to our family. We were never rich but our home never lacked love or a foundation built on trust and loyalty. I will never be able to put into words how very grateful I am. They are my rock and my inspiration. It is because of their sacrifice and great example I am able to share my story with all of you.

THE BET

I had finally reached the place in my life where I put myself first and felt like things were on the rise for the better. To celebrate, I decided to go on a weekend getaway completely unaware that this would be the beginning of a new chapter in my life. My form of relaxation probably differs from most as we all have our own passions and things that bring clarity to us. For me, the competitor inside loves to watch many sports. It's definitely an adrenaline rush for me. So, a few of my buddies and I did just that. We went to Atlantic City to gamble a bit and then we drove to watch UFC 101 which is a mixed martial arts event held in Pennsylvania. At the time I wasn't big into the fight world but I followed the sport here and there. Once we got into the arena to watch the UFC cage fighting I was immediately blown away and all the excitement had my heart pumping in a way I hadn't felt in so long! We sat cage side, the place was electric, and I felt the excitement of all the fans running through my veins. I was finally alive again! It was a huge event where Anderson Silva who is arguably one of the greatest fighters all time, was fighting. His opponent that night was Stephon Bonner. As the fighter's entrance music came on and they walked to the cage, I felt goosebumps crawl up my spine! It was like watching with a different set of eyes in awe and amazement. From that moment on I knew what I wanted to do and what I had to do. That very second I leaned over and said to my buddies sitting next to me, "Hey, I can do this. I want to give it a shot." He looked over to me laughing and said "You are crazy! You had too much red bull and vodka buddy. I'll see you at work on Monday". Little did he know at the time it wasn't the Red bull and Vodka, it was the belief I had in myself. I knew that I could accomplish anything I put my mind to. The adrenaline and passion I felt that night caused me to say goodbye to my comfortable corporate America desk job. With great excitement, I decided to pursue my new dream. One of my closest friends pretty much bet me and called me out on my so called bluff. He said "If you think you can do this I'll bet you." My friend used this proposition to ignite the motivation that was burning within my heart. He had seen flashes of greatness within me and thought this was a good opportunity to re-awaken my sleeping giant. As fate would have it, I ran into a buddy from high school who wrestled with me and was currently competing in mixed martial arts. He affirmed my belief in myself by saying to me "come down to this gym and give it a shot". I was fortunate because he welcomed me with open arms and took me under his wing. At that moment he was a local relatively unknown kid who would soon became my mentor. Being that I started this sport later in life I was happy and grateful to receive all the help I could get. Five plus years later, he beat the very same man I was watching from the audience with excitement. He defeated Anderson Silva, the greatest fighter of all time. The amazing thing is he beat him not once, but twice for the UFC Middleweight Championship! Now everyone in the mixed martial arts world knows Chris Weidman's name. A few years after, Chris Weidman won the belt and I got my big opportunity.

THE MOMENT THAT CHANGED EVERYTHING

Feeling beyond blessed, I was selected to compete in television's Ultimate Fighter Championship Season 19. It felt amazing to be chosen over thousands of fighters all around the world to be a part of history. This was one of the toughest things athletically I had ever done in my life. I had to qualify based on my weight three times in a five-week period. It was really intense. It was great to form bonds with some of the best rising prospects in the world but this wasn't about making friends. The main focus was to fight, give it all I've got, and to see where I end up. I knew I had to put everything I had physically, mentally, and emotionally into this opportunity. Being mentally locked in did not come without sacrifice. Only a select few knew or even realized just how much I had to sacrifice to have the opportunity to fight and get this big break in my life. During preparation for season 19 of Ultimate Fighter, I had to overcome a mountain sized obstacle. During my last sparring session before leaving Vegas, I threw an inside kick and my toe hit the inside knee of my training partner. My toe actually exploded and the bone was actually sticking outside of my skin. I was in incredible pain and agony. Surprisingly, the pain was more emotional than physical. The only thought I had in my head was oh no! Now what am I going to do? How can I even compete? Somehow, I found a way to bite down, grit my teeth, and continue on to my path of greatness. I not only fought in this competition, I actually won it all. Through this epic adventure I, Eddie "Truck" Gordon, won the UFC Ultimate Fighting season 19 championship. The feeling of winning and being on the inside looking out at the fans cheering for me now was indescribable. I was finally HOME! At that moment my name was etched in history forever with only 18 other fighters in the world! My Life completely changed from that moment. Not only did I win the championship, I signed a six-figure contract with the UFC. Even more importantly, it has continued to open up opportunities that I never imagined.

I now have a platform to reach kids and adults just like me who have the drive to be successful. My mission is to let them know that anything is possible if you have passion, a competitive mindset and the determination to succeed in life.

My legacy is not going to be based on how many fights I win, how many houses I own, or how many cars I drive. A true legacy is known by how many people you help and how many lives you transform. I will continue to fulfill this calling and share my story with people all across the world. Thank you for traveling on this journey with me thus far. The following chapters will begin to tap into some of the key ingredients you must have if you want to live a life of greatness. I continue to model my life aspirations after these very factors today. They have transformed my life and if you apply these same elements, I am sure they will lead to amazing breakthroughs in your life as well.

Principle # 4

Opportunity often hides behind adversity. While your storm is raging, be prepared to take advantage of that one opportunity you least expect. It can be the game changer that completely transforms your life.

CHAPTER 5 : THE KEY INGREDIENTS OF SUCCESS

PASSION FUELS THE JOURNEY

The first important ingredient to anyone's success is passion. This is what gives you that incredible excitement and dedication. It's that one defining thing you can't stop thinking about. It literally drives you to wake up in the morning and gives you this indescribable feeling of being alive. Passion is part of what keeps you going when the journey gets tough. There is no such thing as an overnight success. It took many years for me to become what seems like an overnight success to most people today. However, I wouldn't change my path because it has been instrumental to my success and has shaped me into the person I am today. I am here to tell you that you have to do the work when nobody else is watching. The mindset that I've developed and the work that I put in to be successful often went unnoticed. What people recognized was my passion to succeed. My competitive nature drove my inner Truck to excellence in everything I have set out to do. Everything revolved around accomplishing whatever goal it was. This is how you have to be. Your daily activity and lifestyle must be centered around the vision you have for your life. I was very passionate about becoming a professional athlete and I was able to be victorious. Your passion and greatness will attract success to you. It may not come in a day, a week, or even several months. Sometimes it takes a little while. However, it always shows up at the time you really need it the most if you don't give up. My passion fueled me to excel on and off the football field along with any sports arena I stepped into. This is what separates people who win from those who never achieve their full potential. I was not the greatest athlete that ever lived but I achieved big things because my passion guided me. It allowed me to accomplish far more than my God given athletic abilities ever could. The fire still burns today, will burn tomorrow, and will continue to drive me to new levels of success. Your passion is going to push you closer and closer to success in any endeavor you decide to take on. It does not have to be athletics, it can be in business or even in your personal life. Far too often I hear people talk about the obstacles they have to encounter to get where they are going. Successful people know the incredible power of passion. When all else fails, if you have belief and passion for succeeding, you will eventually reach the mountaintop. I will not go down in the record books as an undefeated Fighter but I know that every time I compete I compete with passion and the burning desire to be my very best. You must take this approach in everything you aspire to do in your life. You can't lose when you give it your all, follow your passion, have a vision, and only focus on actions that bring you one step closer to what achievement you are going after. When I lay there exhausted and tired, I know deep down in my heart I left it all out there win lose or draw. It may sound cliche but fighting is just like life. Your success can't be measured by anyone but yourself. Take it personal because it is up to you to shape your destiny. Everyone's version of success is going to be drastically different as well as the outcome but as long as your heart and soul are put forth in any endeavor, your success is inevitable. Fighting is a Microcosm for life and how you fight is going to determine how you live. Just like life, there are many ups as well as downs and the one that comes out on top is the person that masters their will to win.

Do not drown yourself in what if or on negativity. Keep your head up and keep your heart in the game of life at all times. If your heart is filled with passion and a never ending drive to succeed, greatness is sure to follow.

DEVELOP THE MINDSET TO WIN

I don't believe people realize just how important of a role the right mindset plays not just in athletics, but in life in general. Mindset is a key component to any successful story. Without the right mindset, our passion and beliefs can get misguided and backfire against us. What sets my story apart is the fact that through many mistakes, life failures and successes, I found the right mixture of the two. One cannot exist successfully without the other. My whole life I grew up the underdog who was often underappreciated. With me, my life didn't have all the bells and whistles. My advantage over most is the fact that I don't have to be the smartest, fastest, strongest or most athletic. That didn't matter because I was always determined to find a way to win. I will use my strong mental mindset to break through most barriers. When others find a way to quit, I find a way to win. The will to win is not just something you can develop overnight. It takes work along with practice but you can be victorious. Maybe you are the underdog in your life right now. I am a living testimony that you can rise above all of the obstacles you may be facing in your life. You must realize that the mind is the most powerful tool we will ever have at our disposal. Many of us carelessly fail to utilize this weapon because we take it for granted. The stronger your mindset, the more obstacles you can overcome and success will inevitably be yours. When I won Ultimate Fighter I fought guys that were more skilled than me and had much more experience in the sport. I still found a way to take home that championship trophy. A huge reason for that was my mindset. I lost a fight before I claimed the championship but the one thing that never faulted or waivered was my positivity and the need to win. I never once ran from reality. My mindset allowed me to address every roadblock head on and take the right actions to overcome that adversity. It's very important that we continue to grow and develop a winning mindset just like we build our muscles to increase strength. We must be ready to do the things that take us out of our comfort zone because that's when we grow and learn the most. The biggest example I can think of is one of the greatest boxing upsets of all time. That fight I am talking about was Mike Tyson against Buster Douglas. Douglas had no business in the ring that night with Tyson according to everyone else. What they didn't realize is that Buster Douglas had a date with destiny. His mindset was set on success and he would not be denied. He walked into that ring dealing with the death of his mother and he made her a promise that he would do everything in his power to beat Tyson that night. He made good on his promise. No one knew at the time what his mental state was, but he did. He was willing to do whatever it takes to take down the greatest boxer in the world. When Tyson knocked him down everyone in the crowd thought that it was the beginning of the end like most of Tyson's previous opponents. Douglas's mindset going into that fight allowed him to get up and overcome being knocked down. He went on to ultimately shock the world with defeating Mike Tyson and he became the new heavyweight champion of the world. With a winning mindset you too can shock the world and yourself in any arena of your life.

THE LAW OF ACTION

In my early years, I was a huge proponent of the law of attraction. I genuinely believed that if I thought positive and focused on the brighter things in life that the universe would hear my call. This was key to my positive mindset. I was also fortunate enough to have great people in my life and had a conversation with someone I hold in high regard. That person was behavior specialist, Steve Maraboli. Steve helped shape and evolve my mindset with one simple word; action. Now don't get me wrong, I'm a big believer in the law of attraction today but I believe the law needs action behind it to achieve its purpose. My story needed a vision, a place to start and great passion to guide it. When I added action to the equation that was the deciding factor that made my story a success. I believed in myself when no one else did. I had a vision and a belief in myself that was hard for everyone to see or even understand. I heard it all. You're too old, you're too fat, and you're crazy. Why would you leave a safe, comfortable position to fight? What no one else could see was the vision that I had inside my head and on my vision board. That vision would've never become a reality if I did not put action behind it. As you read this I am telling you right now to never allow someone to stop you from pursuing your vision. Thinking positive and making vision boards is a critical part of the process because if you can see it then you can achieve it. After that, once you begin taking the right action its game on. Steve Maraboli helped me clearly understand the law of attraction to where it all made perfect sense to me. We as human beings are addicted to results. Sometimes we don't even realize it but certain things in life force us to change our lifestyles and habits subconsciously. When you're constructing your vision boards and you're thinking positively, you begin to work towards those goals.

Your subconscious mind gets to work letting you know that you need to put the action behind the vision. The law of action is just as important if not more important than the law of attraction. If I don't get up and work and put action towards my goals they will never be accomplished. No matter how positive you think and how many vision boards you create, nothing is going to come to you while you're sitting on your couch at home. We all need a "pop" moment. After speaking with Steve, I had my "pop" moment. That "pop" moment is the sound when your head pops out of your ass and you see the world in a different light. Some point in life we all need to have this defining moment of clarity.

No matter how clear and concise your goals are, you need the driving force of action. Transport your goals and aspirations from your mind onto paper. Writing it down brings those goals into reality and it gives them their power. This can be done on a vision board or just a simple list on a notepad. The importance lies within writing it down. Once it's on paper it becomes real. You have the responsibility of taking action and hitting the ground running. The sooner you get moving the closer you will be to making your vision a reality. You can create a success story for the ages!

Principle #5

Vision, Passion, and Mindset alone will not guarantee success. It takes the discipline of taking the right actions every single day for your success to become a reality!

CHAPTER 6 : LIVE A REGRET FREE LIFE

MY GREATEST FEAR

My biggest fear in life has always been what if. What if I never got stressed out or what if my life never fell apart from under me? What if I just kept going through life sitting at a desk being miserable and unhappy? Too many times we live our lives for other people and we don't pay attention or even focus on ourselves. We try so hard to please them while we completely lose sight of our dreams and aspirations. Life is full of uncertainty. The only guarantee in life is that we all have to leave this earth one day. If I can go through life giving my all and following my dreams, I can lay my head to rest with confidence knowing that I have lived a purpose driven life. You have the opportunity right now to live a life of success and greatness. The pain of regret is far greater than the pain of any obstacle you will ever face on your pathway to excellence.

What would happen if you made a conscious decision to live a regret free life? What opportunities would open up for you? How far would you progress in your life? The possibilities are endless and that alone is exciting! The scariest and most defining moments in a man or woman's life are their last seconds on this earth. As they lay there, this defining conclusion to their life will be met with great peace and satisfaction or, the pain of regret. Nobody wants to look back on their life feeling like they did not live up to their full potential. A regret free life is going to be met with heart ache at times. There may be times where you have to cry. There will be times that you are mentally and physically exhausted. Mistakes will certainly be made. This is all molding and shaping you into who you need to be once you reach the success you truly desire. With all of the challenging experiences, the great successes you experience will far outweigh them. They will lead you to a happy, exciting, and fulfilling life.

THE POWER OF YOUR "WHY"

Unless you have a compelling reason to accomplish your goals, you will not do what it takes to be successful. This is why your why has to be powerful, heartfelt, and personal to you. Your why will be tested each and every day of your life. When your why is fueled with purpose, the how does not hold you captive. You have to want to live a regret free life for yourself. Your spouse, your friends, your family, or I can't do it for you. This is your burning desire and reason for why you are pursuing the goals you have set for yourself. Take it personal.

There will come a moment in time when you feel like giving up. You may even get knocked down but you're going to have to climb back up on that horse. I am here to tell you that when you reach that point in your life where things are at their toughest, tap into your why and ignite your will to win. Remember that you are only a step away from victory. Life is a marathon not a sprint. The first few miles are easy then your body soon gets tired, you begin sweating, and your endurance begins to be tested. Those last several miles before the finish line seem larger than any other miles you have run. It is the same way with your goals and dreams. Push past this moment. Make the decision not to be denied and to fight for your success. In other words, keep on Truckin.

Achieving great success will challenge you in every way

shape and form. The process is filled with obstacles hurdles and adversity. This is why the key ingredients of having a vision, an undying passion, a winning mindset, and a strong desire to take action, are extremely important. With these characteristics you have the power to succeed no matter what stands in your way.

Principle #6

Your dedication, determination, and self-motivation all come from your "WHY". This is what keeps you going when times get tough and when you feel like giving up. It is the driving force behind your life's mission and purpose. Your WHY is your reason for doing what you do.

The one thing I want everyone to remember is that no matter who you are, you have value to give to the world. Within your story lies a message that has the potential to change or even save someone's life. Right now, you can inspire someone to achieve greatness because it is rests inside of us all. Let this message of never giving up, pursuing your dreams, and becoming everything you want to be, ignite the passion that has been buried underneath your surface for far too long. Promise yourself that you will no longer live life on accident. This day, make a vow that you will forever strive to live a life of greatness in whatever it is you do.

I have embraced this journey and now it's time for you to do the same. You owe it to yourself to tap into your full potential and when you reach the crossroads of adversity, always remember to

Keep on Truckin!

ABOUT THE AUTHORS

EDDIE "TRUCK "GORDON

Eddie "Truck" Gordon is a Celebrity NY Emmy Award winning fighter, UFC Ultimate Fighter Champion, a motivational speaker, and life coach. He regularly empowers corporations, fortune 500 companies, and thought leaders in the areas of leadership & personal development. Eddie is also the founder of the Eddie Truck Gordon Foundation whose mission is to help under privileged kids live a life of success, and to put an end to drug abuse.

MEIYOKO TAYLOR

Meiyoko Taylor is a best-selling author, personal development and emotional mastery coach. For over a decade he has helped CEOs, executives, public figures, industry leaders and entrepreneurs maximize their potential through the reconditioning of their mindset. With a strong belief that success in any area starts with your inner world, he has built a practice that focuses on the areas of leadership, neuro-linguistic programming, emotional intelligence, and human excellence.

Made in the USA
San Bernardino, CA
21 December 2017